Our Global Community

Families

Lisa Easterling

Heinemann Library
Chicago, Illinois

Customer Service 888-454-2279
Visit our website at www.heinemannraintree.com

Designed by Joanna Hinton-Malivoire
Photo research by Ruth Smith
Printed and bound in China by South China Printing Co. Ltd.

11 10 09 08 07
10 9 8 7 6 5 4 3 2 1

The Library of Congress has cataloged the first edition of this book as follows:
Easterling, Lisa.
  Families / Lisa Easterling.
    p. cm. -- (Our global community)
  Includes bibliographical references and index.
  ISBN-13: 978-1-4034-9402-3 (hc)
  ISBN-13: 978-1-4034-9411-5 (pb)
 1. Family--Juvenile literature. 2. Family--Cross-cultural studies--Juvenile literature. I. Title.
  HQ519.E37 2007
  306.85--dc22

                    2006034291

Acknowledgements
The publishers would like to thank the following for permission to reproduce photographs: Alamy pp. **4** (Blend Images), **8** (David Sanger Photography), **10** (Creatas), **12** (David Noble Photography), **19**, **20** (Stefan Binkert), **23** (Blend Images); Corbis pp. **5** (Karen Kasmauski), **6** (Ariel Skelley), **7** (ROB & SAS), **9** (George Shelley), **11** (Nik Wheeler), **13** (Dex Images, Inc.), **14** (Ariel Skelley), **15**, **16** (Ariel Skelley), **18**; Getty Images p. **17** (Image Bank).

Cover photograph reproduced with permission of Alamy/J Marshall; Tribaleye Images. Back cover photograph reproduced with permission of Alamy.

Contents

Families Around the World

People have families.

4

People in families care for
each other.

Types of Families

Families are big.

Families are small.

Families live together.

Families live apart.

Families live in houses.

Families move from place to place.

What Families Do Together

Families work together.

Families cook together.

Families play music together.

Families play games together.

Families eat together.

Families read together.

Families walk together.

Families ride bikes together.

Your Family

Families have fun together.

What does your family do?

Family Tree

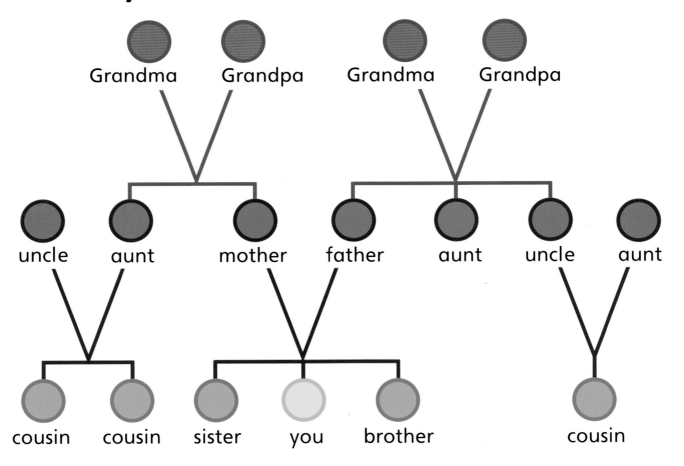

Picture Glossary

 **family** people who care for each other. Families are different everywhere.

Index

Note to Parents and Teachers
This series expands children's horizons beyond their neighborhoods to show that communities around the world share similar features and rituals of daily life. The text has been chosen with the advice of a literacy expert to ensure that beginners can read the books independently or with moderate support. Stunning photographs visually support the text while engaging students with the material.

You can support children's nonfiction literacy skills by helping students use the table of contents, headings, picture glossary, and index.